CONTINENTS IN CLOSE-UP

SOUTH AMERICA
AND ANTARCTICA

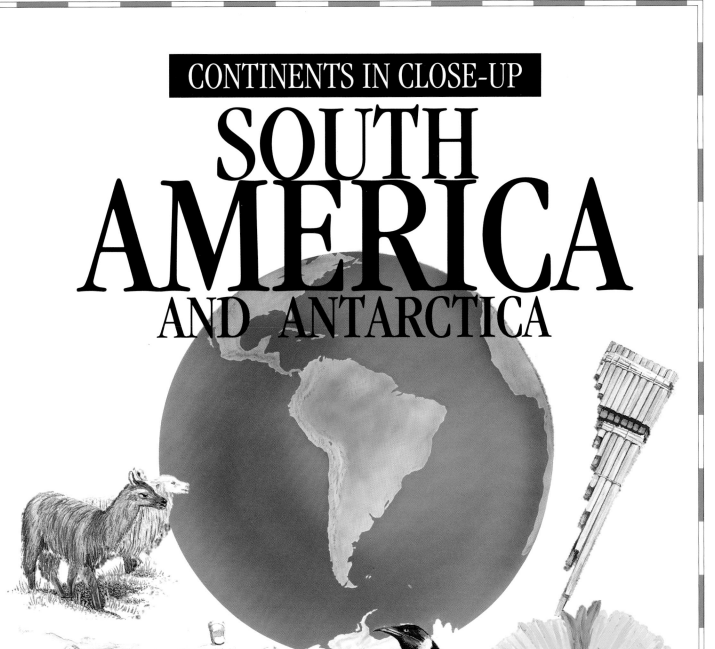

MALCOLM PORTER and KEITH LYE

RAINTREE
STECK-VAUGHN
PUBLISHERS
RSVP®

First published 1999
by Cherrytree Press Limited

First published in the United States 2002
by Raintree Steck-Vaughn Publishers

Library of Congress Cataloging-in-Publication Data

Porter, Malcolm.
  South America and Antarctica / Malcolm Porter
and Keith Lye. p. cm. - - (Continents in close-up)
Originally published: Bath : Cherrytree, 1999, in
series: Continents in close-up. Includes
bibliographical references and index.
  ISBN 0-7398-3239-5
  1. South America - - Juvenile literature.
  2. Antarctica - - Juvenile literature. [1. South
America. 2. Antarctica.] I. Lye, Keith.
  II. Continents in close- up (Austin, Tex.)

F2208.5 .P67 2001
980 - - dc21   2001019561

ISBN 0-7398-3239-5

Printed in Hong Kong

CONTINENTS IN CLOSE-UP

SOUTH AMERICA
AND ANTARCTICA

This illustrated atlas combines maps, pictures, flags, globes,
information panels, diagrams, and charts to give overviews of
the continents of South America and Antarctica and a
closer look at the countries of South America.

COUNTRY CLOSE-UPS

Each double-page spread has these
features:

Introduction The author introduces the
most important facts about the country
or region.

Globes A globe on which you can see the
country's position in the continent and the
world.

Flags Every country's flag is shown.

Information panels Every country has an
information panel, which gives its area,
population and capital, and where
possible its currency, religions, languages,
main towns, and government.

Pictures Important features of each
country are illustrated and captioned to
give a flavor of the country. You can
find out about physical features, famous
people, ordinary people, animals, plants,
places, products, and much more.

Maps Every country is shown on a
clear, accurate map. To get the most out
of the maps it helps to know the symbols,
which are shown in the key on the
opposite page.

Land You can see by the coloring on
the map where the land is forested,
frozen, or desert.

Height Relief hill shading shows where
the mountain ranges are. Individual
mountains are marked by a triangle.

Direction All of the maps are drawn
with north at the top of the page.

Scale All of the maps are drawn to scale
so that you can find the distance
between places in miles or kilometers.

0	200 miles
0	200 kilometers

KEY TO MAPS

PERU	Country name
~~	Country border
	More than 1 million people*
	More than 500,000 people
	Less than 500,000 people
	Country capital
ANDES MTS	Mountain range
Aconcagua 22,869 feet (6960 m)	Mountain with its height

Paraná	River
	Canal
	Lake
	Dam
	Island

	Forest
	Crops
	Dry grassland
	Desert
	Tundra
	Polar

Many large cities, such as Belo Horizonte, have metropolitan populations that are greater than the city figures. Such cities have larger dot sizes to emphasize their importance.

CONTINENT CLOSE-UPS

SOUTH AMERICA

People and Beliefs Map of population densities; chart of percentage of population by country; chart of areas of countries; map of main languages and endangered peoples.

Climate and Vegetation Map of vegetation; chart of land use; maps of temperature and rainfall.

Ecology and Environment Map and panel on environmental damage to land and sea; map, panel, and diagram of volcanoes and other natural hazards; panel on endangered species.

Economy Map of products; chart and panel on gross and per capita national products; map of energy sources.

Politics and History Panel and timeline of great events; map of colonies and dates of independence; map of important historical events.

ANTARCTICA

Antarctica and Islands Map centerd on South Pole showing location of continent and islands; panels and illustrations.

Antarctica and its Exploration Map showing routes of explorers; panel of important dates; map of research stations.

Antarctica Today Map showing mineral resources and areas claimed by various nations; maps of winter and summer temperatures and pack-ice limits; map and panel of the ozone hole; panel on conservation as a World Park.

Index All the names on the maps and in the picture captions can be found in the index at the end of the book.

CONTENTS

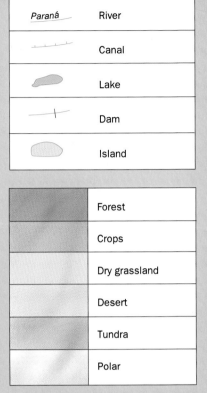

Giant anteater, see page 21

SOUTH AMERICA

South America, the fourth-largest continent, covers about 12 percent of the world's land area. It contains the world's longest mountain range and the world's largest rainforest. The countries of South America contain rich farmland and many other resources, but they are far less developed than Canada and the United States.

Argentina, Brazil, Chile, and Venezuela are the most prosperous countries. Seven independent countries are classified as lower middle-income countries and Guyana is the poorest South American country. South America's population includes Native Americans (Amerindians) and people of European and black African origin. Many people are of mixed descent.

PACIFIC
OCEAN

Simón Bolívar (1783-1830) was a South American military leader. His victories won independence for Bolivia, Colombia, Ecuador, Peru, and Venezuela. Spain and Portugal ruled much of South America between the early 16th and early 19th centuries.

Andean condors are large vultures found in the Andes Mountains. The Andes stretch from Colombia and Venezuela to Cape Horn at the southern tip of South America. They form the world's longest mountain range above sea level.

VENEZUELA

Angel Falls — GUYAN

Guiana Highland

COLOMBIA

ECUADOR

Amazon Basin

ANDES

Atacama Desert

PERU

BOLIVIA

MOUNTAINS

PARAGUAY

CHILE

▲ Aconcagua 22,869 feet (6,960 m)

ARGENTINA

Falkland Islands (UK)

Cape Horn

SOUTH AMERICA
Area: 17,832,000 sq km (6,885,000 sq miles)
Population: 323,924,000
Number of independent countries: 12

SURINAME

FRENCH
GUIANA

*ATLANTIC
OCEAN*

B R A Z I L

*Brazilian
Highlands*

miles
0   500

0   500
kilometers

URUGUAY

Angel Falls, in eastern
Venezuela, is the world's
highest waterfall. It has a
total height of 979 m (3,212 ft)
and a longest single drop of
807 m (2,648 ft). The highlands
of eastern Venezuela form part
of the Guiana Highlands.

Rainforests cover a huge
area of northern South
America. Much of the forest
lies in the Amazon Basin, a
vast area drained by the
Amazon River and its many
tributaries. Large areas of
forest have been cleared.

Llamas are domesticated members
of the camel family. The people of
the Andes use them to carry things
and make their wool into warm
clothing. Llamas do not drink much.
They get moisture from the grasses
and low shrubs that grow in
mountain areas.

Brasília is the capital of Brazil.
Building began in a former
wilderness area in the 1950s.
The city became the official
capital in 1960 and is famous
for its modern buildings. Its
population is small when
compared with those of Rio de
Janeiro and São Paulo. Brazil
is South America's
largest country.

5

VENEZUELA

Venezuela faces the Caribbean Sea, which is part of the Atlantic Ocean. The explorer Christopher Columbus, on his third voyage sailing for Spain, landed on its coast in 1498. Venezuela declared itself independent of Spain in 1811.

The country is one of the world's top 10 producers of oil, which has helped it to develop its economy. Venezuela is one of the more prosperous countries in South America. Although some Venezuelans are rich, many others live in poverty.

VENEZUELA

Area: 912,050 sq km (352,145 sq miles)
Highest point: Pico Bolívar, 5,002 m (16,411 ft)
Population: 22,311,000
Capital: Caracas (pop 2,784,000)
Capital and largest city:
Maracaibo (pop 1,364,000)
Other large city: Valencia (pop 1,032,000)
Official language: Spanish
Religions: Christianity (Roman Catholic 92%), other 8%
Government: Federal republic
Currency: Bolívar

Oil is Venezuela's chief natural resource. Major oil fields lie in the Maracaibo basin, which includes Lake Maracaibo and the plains around it. This basin is one of Venezuela's four land regions. The others are the Andean Highlands, the Guiana Highlands, and the Llanos (tropical grasslands).

Butterflies are common in the rainforests and grasslands of Venezuela. The country's wildlife includes pumas, jaguars, monkeys, sloths, anteaters, crocodiles, and snakes, including the huge anaconda.

Caracas, Venezuela's capital, founded in 1567, was the birthplace of the South American hero Simón Bolívar. Caracas is a modern city, but it has slums on the outskirts. The city lies about 11 km (7 miles) from its port, La Guaira, on the coast.

Caribbean Sea

as Aves Orchila
Los Roques

La Tortuga

Margarita

Porlamar

La Guaira
□ **Caracas**

Maracay

San Juan de
los Morros

Cumaná

Barcelona

Carúpano

Caripito

ATLANTIC
OCEAN

Zaraza

Maturin

Calabozo

Tucupita

s

El Tigre

**San Fernando
de Apure**

Orinoco

**Ciudad
Bolívar**

Ciudad Guayana

Upata

Guri Dam

El Callao

V E N E Z U E L A

Caura

Caroni

Angel Falls

Puerto
Ayacucho

Guiana Highlands

Roraima ▲
9,148 feet
(2,772 m)

miles
0 ————————— 100

0 ————— 100
kilometers

Orinoco

Tourism is a growing
industry. Venezuela has
many beautiful beaches
along the dry, warm
Caribbean coast. Among
many offshore islands is
Margarita, which is noted
for its pearls. About
600,000 tourists visit
Venezuela every year.

Gold and diamonds are
mined in Venezuela, together
with coal, bauxite (aluminium
ore), iron ore, gypsum, and
phosphate rock, which is
used to make fertilizers. But
oil and oil products make up
three-quarters of the country's
exports.

Roraima is the highest peak of
the Guiana Highlands. It reaches
2,772 m (9,904 ft) at the point where
the borders of Venezuela, Guyana,
and Brazil meet. Several rivers rise
in these highlands.

7

THE GUIANAS

Guyana (formerly British Guiana), Suriname (formerly Dutch Guiana), and French Guiana, a French overseas department, are situated in northeastern South America. Together, they are called "the Guianas." They have narrow coastal plains where most of the people live, with plateaus and mountains inland. Guyana is a poor country, but Suriname is more prosperous because of its large bauxite deposits. French Guiana depends largely on financial and administrative support from France.

GUYANA

Area: 214,969 sq km (830,000 sq miles)
Population: 839,000
Capital: Georgetown (pop 200,000)
Official language: English
Religions: Christianity 52%, Hinduism 34%, Islam 9%, other 5%
Government: Republic
Currency: Guyana dollar

SURINAME

Area: 163,265 sq km (63,037 sq miles)
Population: 432,000
Capital: Paramaribo (pop 201,000)
Official language: Dutch
Religions: Christianity 42%, Hinduism 27%, Islam 20%, other 11%
Government: Republic
Currency: Suriname guilder

FRENCH GUIANA

Area: 90,000 sq km (34,749 sq miles)
Population: 153,000
Capital: Cayenne (pop 42,000)
Official language: French
Religions: Christianity 84%, other 16%
Government: French overseas department
Currency: French franc

miles
0   100
0   100
kilometers

•Morawhanna

Charity •

Cuyuni

Georgetown

Bartica •

New Amsterdam

GUYANA

Linden •

Nieuw Nickerie

Berbice

Roraima
9,094 feet (2,772 m) ▲

Essequibo

Courantyne

Apoteri •

Biloku •

Hardwoods are important products in the Guianas. Rainforests containing valuable trees, such as greenheart, cover 90 percent of French Guiana and Suriname and 85 percent of Guyana. The timber industry produces logs and plywood.

Bauxite is the ore from which the metal aluminum is made. Bauxite and aluminum make up more than 70 percent of the exports of Suriname. Guyana also exports bauxite. French Guiana has some bauxite deposits, but they are largely undeveloped.

Georgetown, the capital of Guyana, is built on low coastal land. Strong sea walls and drainage canals prevent flooding of the coastal plain. Only about one-third of the Guyanese live in towns; the rest are farmers.

Macaws, parrots, and other colorful birds live in the rainforests and savanna regions of the Guianas. Among the many animals found in the three countries are caimans, deer, monkeys, ocelots, and tapirs.

ATLANTIC OCEAN

Paramaribo

Groningen

Moengo

Coppename

Marowijne

Mana

Lake Blommestein

Kourou ·

⊡ Cayenne

FRENCH GUIANA (France)

SURINAME

Approuague

St Georges ·

Julianatop
▲ 4,059 feet
(1,230 m)

Tapanahoni

· Saül

· Ouaqui

Sugarcane is one of the main crops of the Guianas. It makes up about one-quarter of the exports of Guyana. The other major crop is rice, which is grown on about three-quarters of the farmland in Suriname. Fishing is another important industry.

Kourou, northwest of Cayenne, the capital of French Guiana, has been the rocket-launching site of the European Space Agency since 1968. France earns money by launching the satellites of other countries.

Brazil

Brazil is the fifth-largest country in the world. Only Russia, Canada, China, and the United States are bigger. The country's main regions are the Amazon Basin, the dry northeast, where farmers rear cattle, and the southeast, Brazil's most thickly populated region. Until 1822 the country was a Portuguese colony. Today Brazil is a rapidly developing country, but many Brazilians are poor. Farming employs 23 percent of the people, and Brazil is one of the world's leading producers of crops and livestock.

BRAZIL

Area: 8,547,403 sq km (3,300,156 sq miles)
Highest point: Pico da Neblina, 3,014 m (9,888 ft)
Population: 161,365,000
Capital: Brasilia (pop, including suburbs, 1,778,000)
Largest cities: São Paulo (pop 16,417,000), Rio de Janeiro (pop 9,888,000), Salvador (pop 2,819,000)
Official language: Portuguese
Religions: Christianity (Roman Catholic 72%, Protestant 23%), other 5%
Government: Federal republic
Currency: Real

Poisonous frogs and various plants contain chemical substances used by the people of the Amazon for hunting and medicines. Curare, a drug used in anesthetics, comes from the Amazon. Other useful substances, as yet undiscovered, may also exist in the rainforest.

▲ Pico da Neblina
9,888 feet (3,014 m)

Negro

Japurá

Amazon

Manaus

Japurá

Amazon

A m a z o n   B a s i n

Purus

Madeira

Tapajós

Jurua

Pôrto Velho

Rio Branco

Mato Grosso
Plateau

Cuiabá

Native Americans live in decreasing numbers in the vast rainforests of the Amazon Basin. Many have given up their traditional way of life and now work in mines. The future of these people is threatened because their forest home is being destroyed. Some groups have already died out.

•Corumbá

Iguaçu
Falls

Uruguay

Uruguaiana
Bagé

Cars, aircraft, chemicals, processed food, iron and steel, paper, and textiles are leading industries in Brazil. The country's rich mineral reserves include bauxite, chrome, diamonds, gold, iron ore, manganese, and tin.

Amazon Basin The world's second-longest river after the Nile, the Amazon has more water than any other. The Amazon Basin contains the world's largest rainforest. In recent years, about one-tenth of the forest has been destroyed. Plants and animals are vanishing before scientists have had a chance to study them.

Calçoene

Macapá

Marajo Island

Belém

São Luís

Parnaíba

Fortaleza

Teresina

Juàzeiro do Norte

Natal

São Francisco

Recife

Maceió

Aracaju

B R A Z I L

Araguaia

Tocantins

Xingu

Salvador

Brasília

ATLANTIC OCEAN

Goiânia

Montes Claros

Paraná

Uberaba

Belo Horizonte

Vitória

miles

0   400

0   400

kilometers

Ribeirão Prêto

Maringâ

Campinas

Ponta Grossa   **São Paulo**   **Rio de Janeiro**

Curitiba

Passo Fundo

Florianópolis

Caxias do Sul

Santa Maria

Pôrto Alegre

Rio Grande

Sloths are strange hairy mammals that live in the forests. They use their hook-like claws to hang upside down from branches and rarely move except to reach more of the leaves on which they continuously feed. They remain so still that lichens and mosses grow on their fur.

Sugar Loaf Mountain is a landmark of Rio de Janeiro, Brazil's second-largest city. The city has magnificent scenery and is famous for its beaches, nightlife, and colorful carnivals.

11

COLOMBIA

Colombia, in the northwest corner of the continent, is South America's fourth-largest country. In the north, it faces the Caribbean Sea, an arm of the Atlantic Ocean. The Pacific Ocean lies to the west. Colombia has three main regions, including the northern part of the Andes Mountains. Coastal plains lie to the north and west. The southeast contains forested plains, which are drained by tributaries of the Orinoco and Amazon rivers.

The country was the heart of the Spanish colony of New Granada, which also included Venezuela, Ecuador, and Panama in Central America. It achieved independence in 1819.

COLOMBIA

Area: 1,138,914 sq km (439,737 sq miles)
Highest point: Cristóbal Colón, 5,775 m (18,947 ft)
Population: 37,541,000
Capital and largest city: Bogotá (pop 5,026,000)
Other large cities: Cali (pop 1,719,000), Medellín (pop 1,621,000)
Official language: Spanish
Religions: Christianity (Roman Catholic 95%), other 5%
Government: Republic
Currency: Peso

Statues and other carvings were made by the Chibcha people, who founded a major civilization in the Andes region. Spanish inraders conquered the Chibcha between 1536 and 1538. Spain introduced Roman Catholicism and ruled the country until 1819, when Simón Bolívar's army defeated Spanish forces in a battle.

Coffee is Colombia's leading export crop. Other exports include oil, chemicals, wood and fish products, textiles, and coal. Agriculture employs 27 percent of the people. Cattle are raised, and crops include bananas, cotton, rice, and sugarcane.

Bogotá, capital of Colombia, stands on a high plateau surrounded by mountains in the eastern Andes. The Spanish conquerors of the Chibcha founded the city in 1538. The Andes region is the home of about three-quarters of the population of Colombia.

Coca is a native plant of Colombia. The leaves of some types of coca are used to make cocaine, a drug that is illegally exported to the United States and other countries. The cocaine trade brings great wealth to the drug dealers as well as violence and hardship.

Jaguars once lived all over South America. Now they are found only in the most isolated areas of forest and in national parks. They are the largest of the wild cats found in the Americas, but overhunting and deforestation threaten their survival.

Emeralds were once traded by the Chibcha people. Today, Colombia produces about four-fifths of the world's emeralds. Colombia also produces coal, gold, oil and natural gas, and salt, which is used in the country's large chemical industry.

Meta

Puerto Carreño

Orinoco

B I A

Inírida

Putumayo

Leticia

ECUADOR

Ecuador lies on the equator. Its name comes from the Spanish word meaning "equator." The country's main regions are the hot coastal lowlands, the Andes Mountains, and the humid eastern plains, which are drained by the Amazon and its tributaries.

The Incas conquered the region that is now Ecuador in the late 15th century. In turn, the Spanish defeated the Incas in 1534. Ecuador became independent in 1822.

Marine iguanas, giant tortoises, and other unique animals live on Ecuador's Galapagos Islands, which lie about 1,000 km (1,600 miles) off the coast. The naturalist Charles Darwin studied the islands' animals and plants and used his observations to develop his theory of evolution.

ECUADOR

Area: 283,561 sq km (109,484 sq miles)
Highest point: Chimborazo, 6,267 m (20,561 ft)
Population: 11,698,000
Capital: Quito (pop 1,488,000)
Largest cities: Guayaquil (pop 1,974,000), Cuenca (255,000)
Official language: Spanish
Religions: Christianity (Roman Catholic 93%), other 7%
Government: Republic
Currency: Sucre

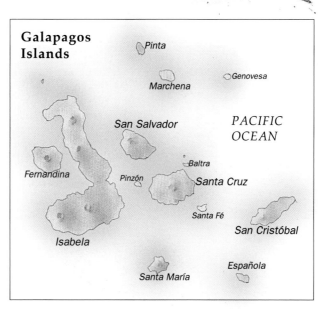

Galapagos Islands

Pinta

Marchena

Genovesa

San Salvador

PACIFIC OCEAN

Baltra

Fernandina

Pinzón

Santa Cruz

Santa Fé

San Cristóbal

Isabela

Santa María

Española

Bahía de Caráquez

Manta

Portoviejo

Jipijapa

PACIFIC OCEAN

Fishing is an important industry in the coastal waters, where herring and mackerel are caught. Shrimp is another important seafood and is increasingly farmed in ponds.

Cotopaxi, south of the capital city, Quito, is one of the world's highest active volcanoes at 5,897 m (19,347 ft). When it erupted in 1877, avalanches of mud, caused by melting snow mixing with volcanic ash, buried large areas. Around 1,000 people were killed. Ecuador has more than 30 active volcanoes.

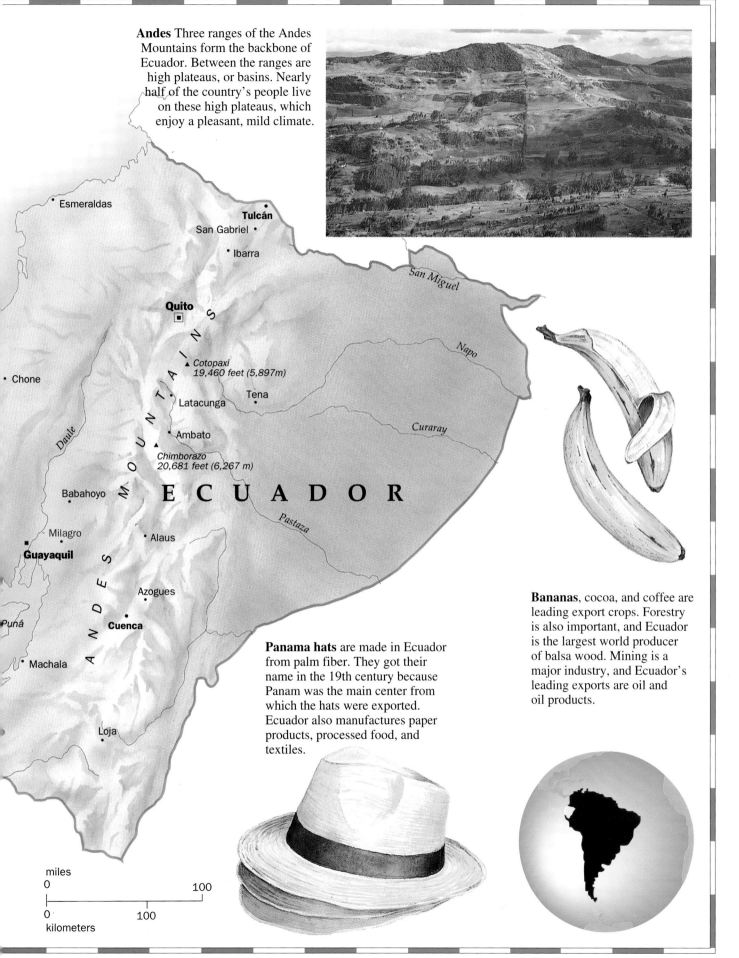

Andes Three ranges of the Andes Mountains form the backbone of Ecuador. Between the ranges are high plateaus, or basins. Nearly half of the country's people live on these high plateaus, which enjoy a pleasant, mild climate.

Esmeraldas

Tulcán
San Gabriel

Ibarra

San Miguel

Quito

Napo

Chone

Cotopaxi
19,460 feet (5,897m)

Tena

Latacunga

Curaray

Daule

Ambato

Chimborazo
20,681 feet (6,267 m)

E C U A D O R

Babahoyo

Pastaza

Milagro

Alaus

Guayaquil

Puná

Azogues

Cuenca

Machala

Bananas, cocoa, and coffee are leading export crops. Forestry is also important, and Ecuador is the largest world producer of balsa wood. Mining is a major industry, and Ecuador's leading exports are oil and oil products.

Panama hats are made in Ecuador from palm fiber. They got their name in the 19th century because Panam was the main center from which the hats were exported. Ecuador also manufactures paper products, processed food, and textiles.

Loja

M O U N T A I N S
A N D E S

miles
0   100
0   100
kilometers

PERU

Behind the narrow, dry coastal plain of Peru lie the Andes Mountains, which contain active volcanoes and high plateaus between the ranges. East of the Andes are plains covered by rainforests. From about AD 1200, Peru was the heart of the great Inca civilization. Spanish soldiers conquered Peru in the 1520s and finally conquered the Incas in 1533. Peru became independent from Spain in 1821. Native Americans now make up nearly half of the population and the Inca language, Quechua, is one of Peru's two official languages.

PERU

Area: 1,285,216 sq km (496,225 sq miles)
Highest point: Huarascarán, 6,768 m (22,205 ft)
Population: 24,288,000
Capital and largest city: Lima (pop 5,706,000)
Other large cities: Arequipa (pop 619,000), Callao (615,000)
Official languages: Spanish, Quechua
Religions: Christianity (Roman Catholic 92%, Protestant 5%), other 3%
Government: Republic
Currency: Nuevo sol

Toucans are tropical birds of Central and South America. There are many different kinds, all with large, brightly colored bills. Some are found in Peru's eastern forests, where they gather in small flocks high in the trees.

Machu Picchu, an ancient Inca city, stands on a peak in south-central Peru. The Incas ruled one of the largest Native American empires. At its height, the empire stretched from southern Colombia, through Ecuador and Peru, into Chile and Argentina.

miles
0 _____ 200
0 _____ 200
kilometers

Talara
Sullana
Piura Chulucanas
Marañón

P   A   E   R   U
N
D   Ucayali
Chiclayo
Bellavista
E
Huallaga
S
Trujillo
Pucallpa
Huarascarán
22,205 feet (6,768 m)
Chimbote
Huaraz
Huánuco
M
Cerro de Pasco
O
Huacho
U
Huaral
N
Callao Lima   Huancayo
T

Huanta
Ayacucho

Ica

Nazca

PACIFIC
OCEAN

Lima, Peru's capital, lies just inland from its port of Callao. Manufacturing is small-scale in Peru. Farming is the main occupation, and mining is also important. Copper is the country's chief export. Peru also produces oil, silver, zinc, and other minerals.

Iquitos

Amazon

Huge patterns and drawings of animals are marked on the desert floor at Nazca, in southern Peru. Some are 2 km (1.2 miles) long and completely visible only from the air. Nobody knows the significance of these ancient markings or who made them, but archaeologists think they may have had a religious or astronomical purpose.

Source of the Amazon The mighty Amazon River rises in the Peruvian Andes in a small stream called the Apurimac. The Apurimac eventually flows into the Ucayali River, which flows north to join the Marañón River. From here the Amazon flows east to the Atlantic Ocean.

Urubamba

Machu
Picchu

Cuzco

Apurimac

Puerto
Maldonado

Lake Titicaca, the world's highest navigable lake, lies on Peru's border with Bolivia. It occupies a basin between ranges of the Andes Mountains, at 3,812 m (12,507 ft) above sea level. Local people use reed boats to sail on the lake.

Juliaca

Puno

Arequipa

Lake
Titicaca

Mollendo

Tacna

BOLIVIA

Bolivia is a landlocked country that is one of the poorest in South America. It contains part of the Andes Mountains, together with forested plains in the north and east. Native Americans have lived in the area for about 10,000 years. The main groups today are the Aymara and the Quechua. Both languages are official, with Spanish. Bolivian culture, like that of much of South America, is a mix of local and European influences.

BOLIVIA

Area: 1,098,581 sq km (424,165 sq miles)
Highest point: Nevado Sajama, 6,542 m (21,463 ft)
Population: 7,588,000
Capital: La Paz (actual), Sucre (official)
Largest cities: La Paz (pop 785,000), Santa Cruz (pop 767,000), Cochabamba (pop 449,000)
Official languages: Spanish, Aymara, Quechua
Religions: Christianity (Roman Catholic 89%, Protestant 10%), other 1%
Government: Republic
Currency: Boliviano

Potatoes and wheat are grown on the Altiplano, a plateau between the eastern and western ranges of the Andes. Bananas, cocoa, coffee, and maize are grown at lower, warmer levels. Agriculture employs about 47 percent of Bolivia's people.

Tin is mined in Bolivia, a country rich in minerals, including oil, gold, and silver. Bolivia exports minerals, but it has few manufacturing industries. Soya beans and timber are also exported.

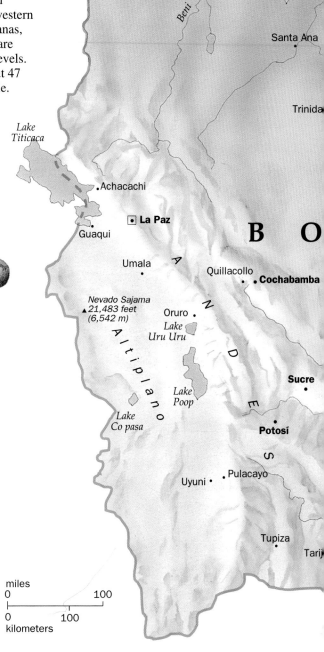

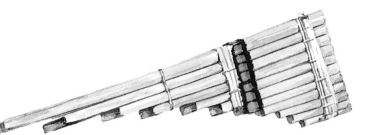

Reed pipes and flutes are played by Native American musicians in the Andes. Their haunting music is played at traditional festivals.

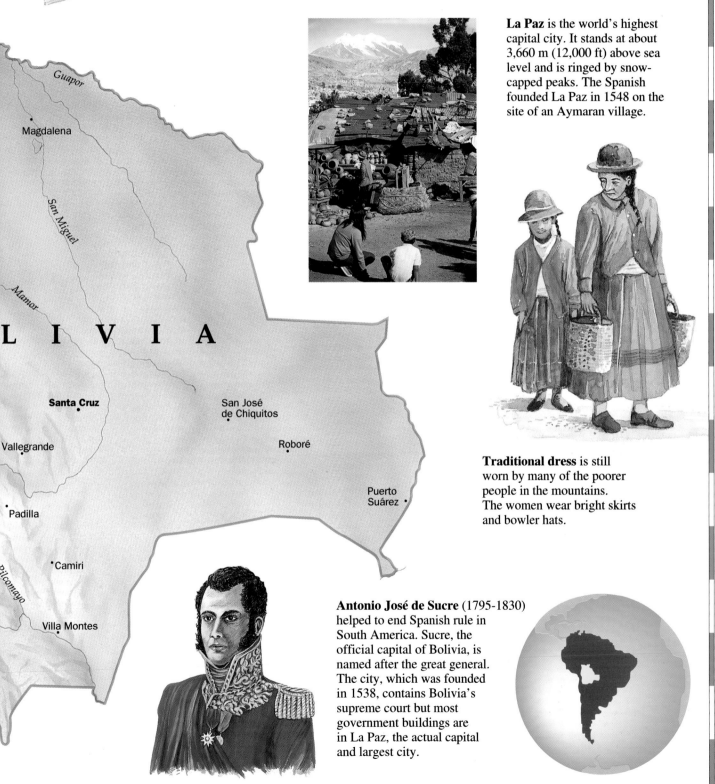

La Paz is the world's highest capital city. It stands at about 3,660 m (12,000 ft) above sea level and is ringed by snow-capped peaks. The Spanish founded La Paz in 1548 on the site of an Aymaran village.

Traditional dress is still worn by many of the poorer people in the mountains. The women wear bright skirts and bowler hats.

Guapor

Magdalena

San Miguel

Mamor

L I V I A

Santa Cruz

San José de Chiquitos

Vallegrande

Roboré

Padilla

Puerto Suárez

Camiri

pilcomayo

Villa Montes

Antonio José de Sucre (1795-1830) helped to end Spanish rule in South America. Sucre, the official capital of Bolivia, is named after the great general. The city, which was founded in 1538, contains Bolivia's supreme court but most government buildings are in La Paz, the actual capital and largest city.

PARAGUAY

Paraguay is a landlocked country. Rivers make up most of its boundaries. The land consists mostly of large plains, plateaus, and hills. The climate is warm and humid. Most people live in the east. Paraguay's earliest-known people were Native Americans called the Guaraní. The Guaraní language is now one of the country's two official languages. Most of the people in Paraguay are mestizos of mixed Native American and European origin.

PARAGUAY

Area: 406,752 sq km (150,048 sq miles)
Highest point: 680 m (2,231 ft), in the southeast
Population: 4,955,000
Capital and largest city:
Asunción (pop 502,000)
Other large city: San Lorenzo (133,000)
Official languages: Spanish, Guaraní
Religions: Christianity (Roman Catholic 88%, Protestant 5%), other 7%
Government: Republic
Currency: Guaraní

Gauchos are cowboys who work on ranches in Paraguay and elsewhere on the grassy plains called pampas. Farming employs about half of Paraguay's people. Soya bean flour, cotton, oilseed cakes, vegetable oils, meat, and hides are leading exports.

Gran Chaco

Bahía Neg

Fortín Coronel
Eugenio Garay

Mariscal
Estigarribia

P A R A G U

Verde

Monte Lindo

Pilcomayo

miles
0 ———————————————— 100

0 ———————— 100
kilometers

Pila

Hydroelectric power stations provide Paraguay with abundant electricity. Paraguay shares the huge Itaipú Dam with Brazil. When it was completed in 1991, this dam became one of the world's largest.

Giant anteaters feed on the plentiful supplies of ants and termites found in the humid forests and plains. The animals tear open the anthills with their strong claws and lick up the ants. They have a long, sticky tongue but no teeth.

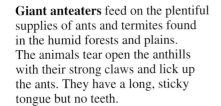

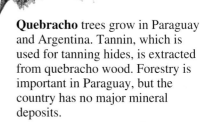

Quebracho trees grow in Paraguay and Argentina. Tannin, which is used for tanning hides, is extracted from quebracho wood. Forestry is important in Paraguay, but the country has no major mineral deposits.

Asunción, capital of Paraguay, was founded by Spanish settlers in 1537 at the junction of the Paraguay and Pilcomayo rivers. Asunción is the country's main industrial city. Manufactured products include cement, processed food, leather goods, and textiles.

Soccer is Paraguay's most popular sport. It is played throughout much of South America, especially in Argentina, Brazil, and Uruguay, which have distinguished records in international soccer competitions.

Fuerte Olimpo

Puerto Sastre

Puerto Casado

Puerto Pinasco

Pedro Juan Caballero

A Y

Paraguay

Horqueta

Concepción

San Pedro

Salto del Guairá

Rosario

Asunción

San Lorenzo

San Bernardino

Itaipú Dam

Paraguari

Ciudad del Este

Villarrica

Lake Ver

Caazapá

San Ignacio

Paran

Encarnación

CHILE

Chile has an unusual shape. It is more than 10 times as long as it is wide. Its eastern borders run through the high Andes Mountains. To the west the land descends through valleys and basins to the coastal plain along the Pacific Ocean. In the north is the bleak Atacama Desert. In the center is the Central Valley, which has hot, dry summers and mild, rainy winters. This region contains three-quarters of the population. To the south, it gets colder and rainier. The far south is one of the world's stormiest places.

Mestizos make up about 75 percent of Chile's population and people of European descent 20 percent. Native Americans make up only 3 percent of the population. Until 1818 most of the country was a colony of Spain.

CHILE

Area: 756,626 sq km (292,135 sq miles)
Highest point: Ojos del Salado, 6,880 m (22,572 ft)
Population: 14,419,000
Capital and largest city: Santiago (pop 5,077,000)
Other large cities: Concepción (pop 350,000), Viña del Mar (pop 322,000)
Official language: Spanish
Religions: Christianity (Roman Catholic 77%, Protestant 13%), other 10%
Government: Republic
Currency: Peso

Atacama Desert This desert is one of the driest in the world. It stretches about 1,700 km (1,056 miles) south from the Peruvian border. The region has rich deposits of copper and of sodium nitrate, which are used to make explosives and fertilizers.

Grapes are grown in the warm Central Valley. Chile is an important producer of wines. Agriculture employs 19 percent of the people. Major crops include beans, fruits, maize, and wheat. Farmers also keep cattle, sheep, and other animals.

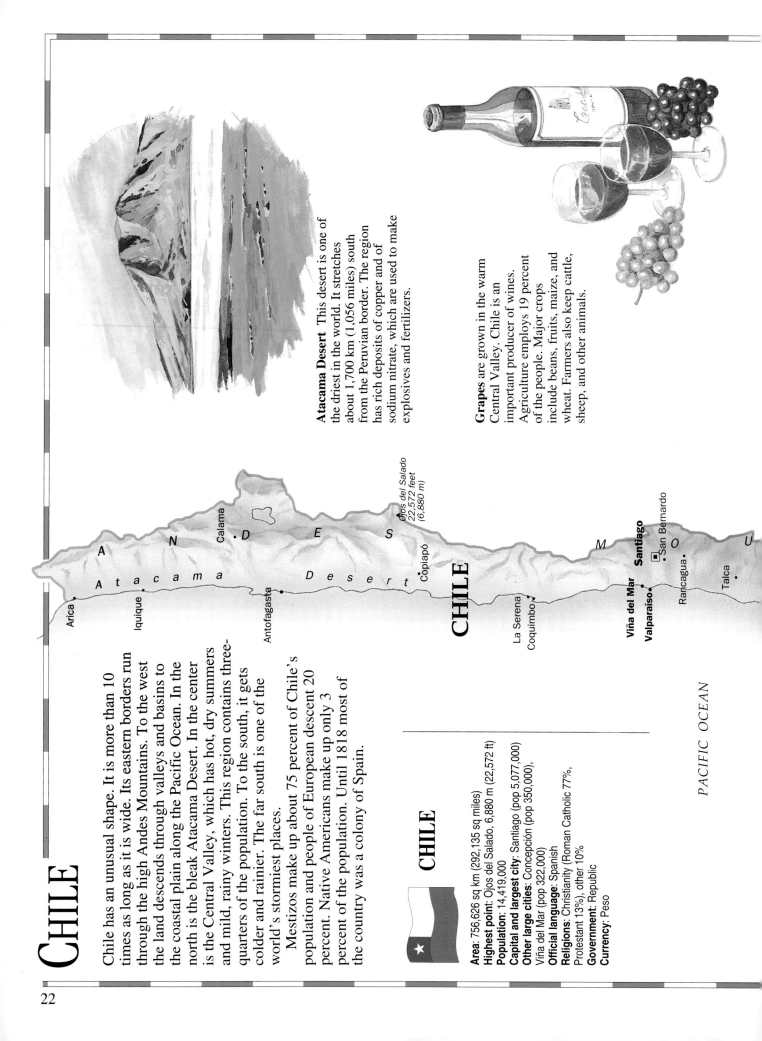

Ojos del Salado
22,572 feet
(6,880 m)

Calama

A   N   D   E   S

Copiapó

Arica

Iquique

Atacama   Desert

Antofagasta

CHILE

La Serena

Coquimbo

Viña del Mar

Valparaíso

M

Santiago

San Bernardo

O

Rancagua

Talca

U

PACIFIC OCEAN

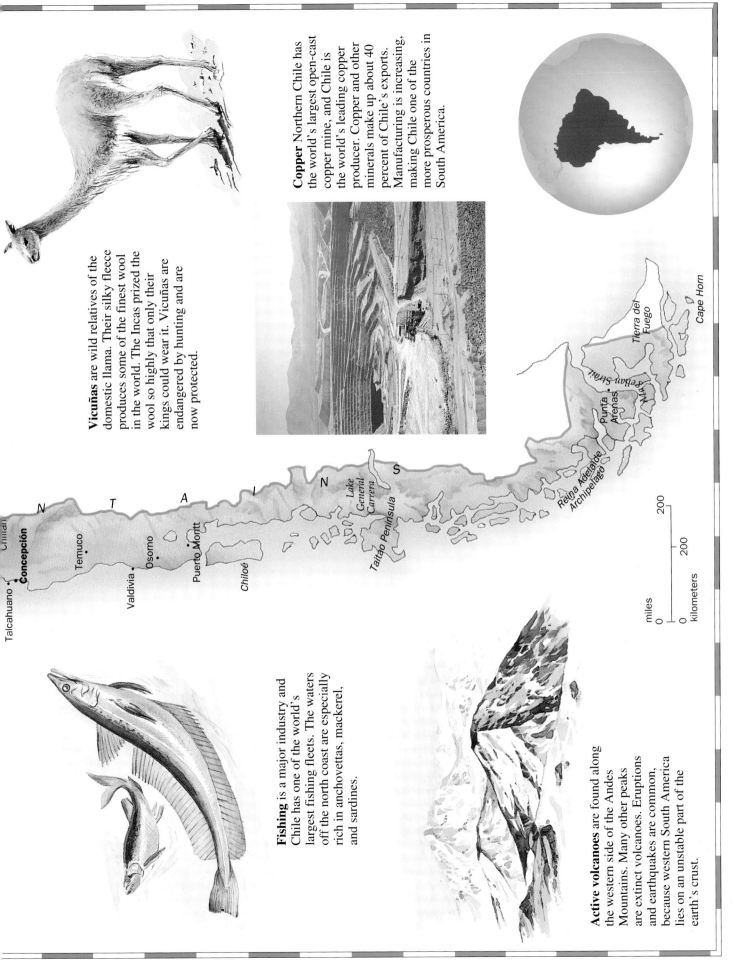

Vicuñas are wild relatives of the domestic llama. Their silky fleece produces some of the finest wool in the world. The Incas prized the wool so highly that only their kings could wear it. Vicuñas are endangered by hunting and are now protected.

Copper Northern Chile has the world's largest open-cast copper mine, and Chile is the world's leading copper producer. Copper and other minerals make up about 40 percent of Chile's exports. Manufacturing is increasing, making Chile one of the more prosperous countries in South America.

Fishing is a major industry and Chile has one of the world's largest fishing fleets. The waters off the north coast are especially rich in anchovettas, mackerel, and sardines.

Active volcanoes are found along the western side of the Andes Mountains. Many other peaks are extinct volcanoes. Eruptions and earthquakes are common, because western South America lies on an unstable part of the earth's crust.

Talcahuano

Chillán

Concepción

Temuco

Valdivia

Osorno

Puerto Montt

Chiloé

Taitao Peninsula

Lake General Carrera

Reina Adelaide Archipelago

Punta Arenas

Magellan Strait

Tierra del Fuego

Cape Horn

N T A I N S

miles 0 200

kilometers 0 200

ARGENTINA

Argentina is the second-largest country in South America. The Andes Mountains lie in the west. In the center and north lie large plains, with the fertile pampas region in east-central Argentina, near the capital, Buenos Aires. In the south, the Andes overlook a plateau region called Patagonia. At the tip of Argentina lies the island of Tierra del Fuego, separated from the mainland by the Magellan Strait, which links the Atlantic and Pacific oceans. The weather is warm and wet in the north and cold and dry in the south.

Until 1816 Argentina was part of a Spanish colony. About 85 percent of the people are of European descent. Mestizos make up most of the remaining 15 percent.

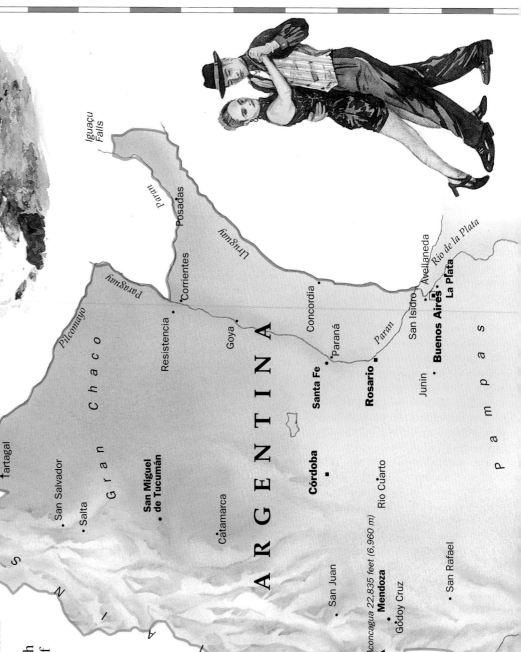

Iguaçu Falls These magnificent falls lie on the Iguaçu River on the Argentina-Brazil border. The falls are about 4 km (2.2 miles) wide and up to 82 m (269 ft) high.

ARGENTINA

Area: 2,780,400 sq km (1,073,519 sq miles)
Highest point: Aconcagua, 6,960 m (22,835 ft)
Population: 35,220,000
Capital and largest city: Buenos Aires (pop 10,990,000)
Other large cities: Córdoba (pop 1,198,000), Rosario (pop 1,096,000)
Official language: Spanish
Religions: Christianity (Roman Catholic 91%), other 9%
Government: Republic
Currency: Peso

Aconcagua, an extinct volcano in the Andes close to the border with Chile, is the highest peak in North and South America. It reaches a height of 6,960 m (22,835 ft) above sea level.

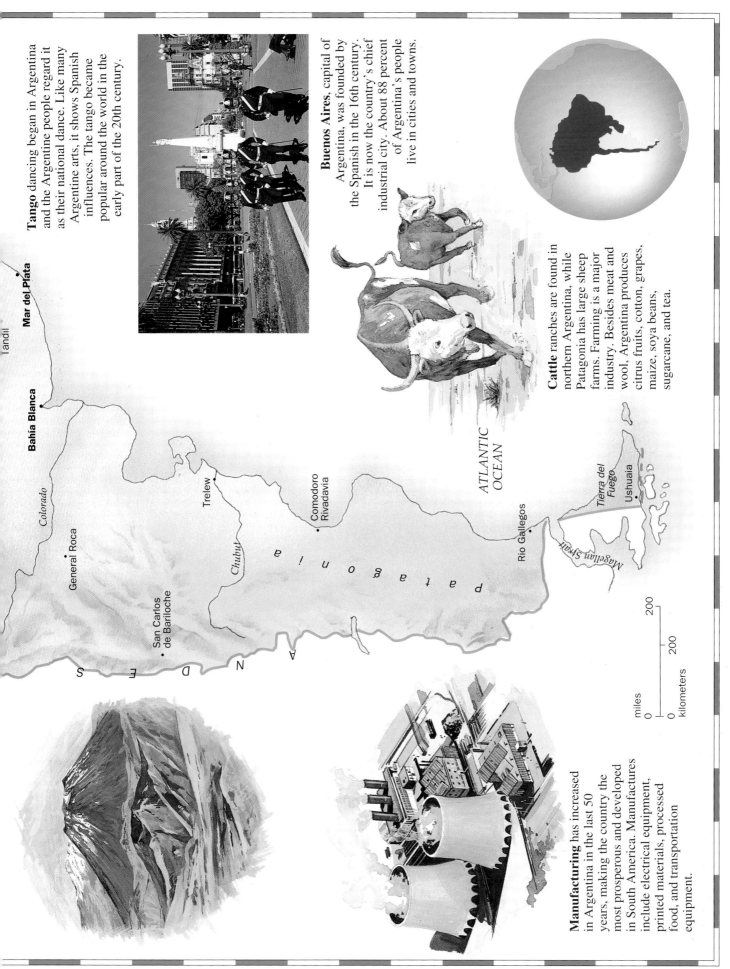

Tango dancing began in Argentina and the Argentine people regard it as their national dance. Like many Argentine arts, it shows Spanish influences. The tango became popular around the world in the early part of the 20th century.

Buenos Aires, capital of Argentina, was founded by the Spanish in the 16th century. It is now the country's chief industrial city. About 88 percent of Argentina's people live in cities and towns.

Cattle ranches are found in northern Argentina, while Patagonia has large sheep farms. Farming is a major industry. Besides meat and wool, Argentina produces citrus fruits, cotton, grapes, maize, soya beans, sugarcane, and tea.

ATLANTIC OCEAN

Mar del Plata

Tandil

Bahía Blanca

Colorado

General Roca

San Carlos de Bariloche

A N D E S

Chubut

Trelew

Comodoro Rivadavia

P a t a g o n i a

Rio Gallegos

Magellan Strait

Tierra del Fuego

Ushuaia

miles
0

kilometers
0

200

200

Manufacturing has increased in Argentina in the last 50 years, making the country the most prosperous and developed in South America. Manufactures include electrical equipment, printed materials, processed food, and transportation equipment.

URUGUAY

Uruguay is South America's second smallest independent country, after Suriname. It is a land of grassy plains and hills.

About 90 percent of the people now live in cities and towns. Native Americans once occupied Uruguay, but only a few Amerindians remain. The country was part of a Spanish colony until 1828. People of European descent make up 86 percent of the population, mestizos 8 percent, and descendants of black Africans 6 percent.

Textiles are among the leading manufactures produced in Uruguay. Other manufactures include beer, cement, and processed food. Uruguay is one of the more prosperous of the developing countries in South America.

URUGUAY

Area: 177,414 sq km (68,500 sq miles)
Highest point: Mirador Nacional, 501 m (1,644 ft)
Population: 3,203,000
Capital and largest cities: Montevideo (pop 1,379,000)
Other large cities: Salto (80,000) Paysand (76,000)
Official language: Spanish
Religions: Christianity (Roman Catholic 78%, Protestant 8%), other 14%
Government: Republic
Currency: Peso

Livestock farming is the most valuable form of agriculture in Uruguay. Sheep and cattle ranches make up four-fifths of the land. Major products include beef, hides and leather goods, and wool. Crops include maize, potatoes, sugar beets, and wheat.

Salto

Uruguay

Paysandú

Paso de los Toros

Negro

Fray Bentos

Mercedes

Dolores

Trinidad

Río de la Plata

Montevideo, Uruguay's capital and chief port, stands on the coast where the Rio de la Plata estuary meets the Atlantic Ocean. Founded in 1726, Montevideo and its suburbs contain most of Uruguay's industries.

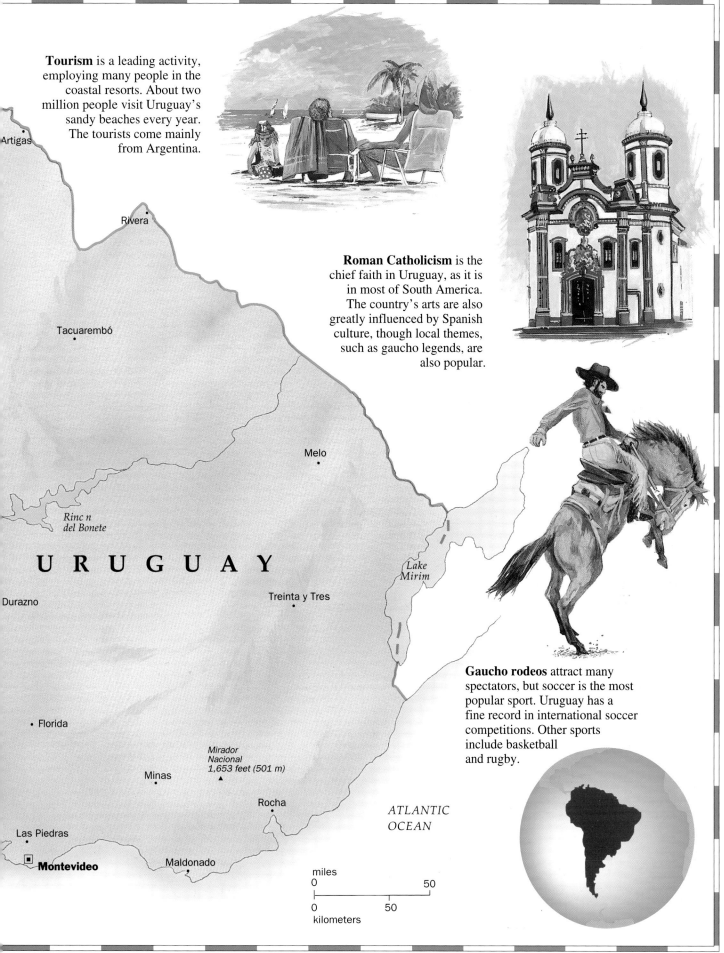

Tourism is a leading activity, employing many people in the coastal resorts. About two million people visit Uruguay's sandy beaches every year. The tourists come mainly from Argentina.

Artigas

Rivera

Tacuarembó

Roman Catholicism is the chief faith in Uruguay, as it is in most of South America. The country's arts are also greatly influenced by Spanish culture, though local themes, such as gaucho legends, are also popular.

Melo

Rinc n del Bonete

U R U G U A Y

Lake Mirim

Durazno

Treinta y Tres

Gaucho rodeos attract many spectators, but soccer is the most popular sport. Uruguay has a fine record in international soccer competitions. Other sports include basketball and rugby.

• Florida

Mirador Nacional 1,653 feet (501 m) ▲

Minas

Rocha

ATLANTIC OCEAN

Las Piedras

◻ **Montevideo**

Maldonado

miles
0 — 50

0 — 50
kilometers

PEOPLE AND BELIEFS

South America contains between five and six percent of the world's population.
Large parts of the continent are nearly empty of people. They include
the Amazon Basin, the Atacama Desert, and Patagonia.
One densely populated region includes southeastern
Brazil and northeastern Argentina. It contains
the continent's largest cities: São Paulo
and Rio de Janeiro in Brazil and
Buenos Aires in Argentina.
Parts of the high plateaus
in the Andes Mountains
and also central Chile
are thickly
populated.

Population Densities

Number of people
per square kilometer

Over 100

Between 50 and 100

Between 10 and 50

Between 1 and 10

Below 1

Main Cities

■ Cities of more than
1,000,000 people

● Cities of more than
500,000 people

Rainforest peoples
traditionally believe in a
world of spirits that live
in people, animals, and
plants. Boys, and
sometimes girls, may
undergo initiation rites
to mark their adulthood.

Population and Area

Brazil, one of the world's largest countries, is larger than the entire continent of Australia. Brazil and Argentina are the two giants of South America. They make up more than three-fifths of the area of the continent and contain about three-fifths of its population. Suriname is the smallest independent country, though French Guiana is even smaller.

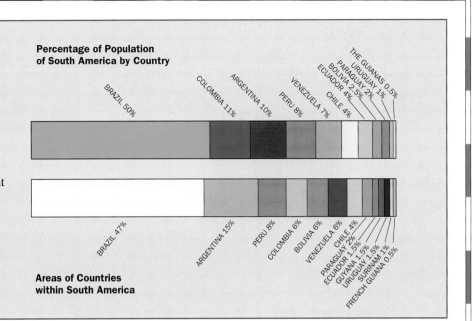

Percentage of Population of South America by Country

BRAZIL 50% · COLOMBIA 11% · ARGENTINA 10% · PERU 8% · VENEZUELA 7% · CHILE 4% · ECUADOR 4% · BOLIVIA 2.5% · PARAGUAY 2% · URUGUAY 1% · THE GUIANAS 0.5%

BRAZIL 47% · ARGENTINA 15% · PERU 8% · COLOMBIA 6% · BOLIVIA 6% · VENEZUELA 6% · CHILE 4% · PARAGUAY 2% · ECUADOR 2% · GUYANA 1.5% · URUGUAY 1.5% · SURINAM 1% · FRENCH GUIANA 0.5%

Areas of Countries within South America

South Americans and religions

The first South Americans were descended from people who migrated from the north through Central America. As they moved south, they formed many groups, each with its own language and customs.

European settlers, who began to arrive in the early 16th century, forced the Native Americans to work for them. They also imported black slaves from Africa. Millions died of harsh treatment and illnesses, such as influenza and measles, which the settlers brought with them. Only Bolivia, Peru and Ecuador still have large groups of Native Americans. Many other South Americans are mestizos, of mixed Native American and European descent.

As well as diseases, the European settlers brought with them the Christian religion. Missionaries forced the people to abandon their traditional gods and beliefs. Today most South Americans (over 90%) are Roman Catholics but an increasing number belong to Protestant churches.

Languages

Most of the people of South America speak Spanish or–in Brazil–Portuguese. English is spoken in Guyana, Dutch in Suriname, French in French Guiana. Quechua, Aymara and Guaraní are Native American languages that have survived in Peru, Bolivia, and Paraguay. Other traditional languages are also spoken by small groups of Native Americans. The survival of some of the peoples shown on the map is threatened.

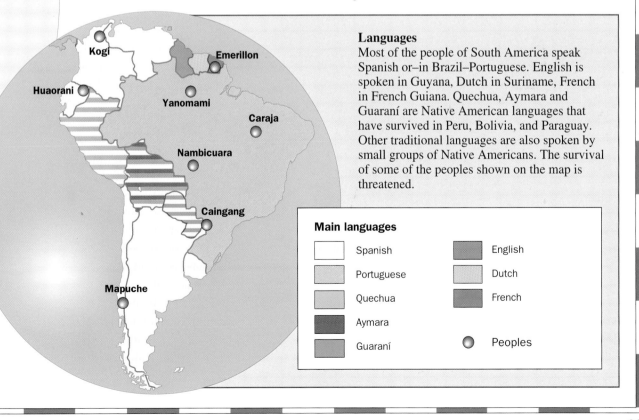

Main languages

- Spanish
- Portuguese
- Quechua
- Aymara
- Guaraní
- English
- Dutch
- French
- Peoples

CLIMATE AND VEGETATION

South America extends from the steamy, hot tropical regions in the north to the cold windswept island of Tierra del Fuego in the far south.
The continent also includes the Atacama Desert, which extends along the coast of Peru and northern Chile. One of the driest places on Earth, parts of it have had no rainfall for 400 years. Patagonia, in southern Argentina, is another dry region.

In the Andes Mountains, the climate changes the higher one goes. Tropical forests grow on the lower slopes near the equator. But higher up are cold pastures overlooked by snow-capped peaks.

- Mountain
- Tundra
- Mixed forest
- Evergreen forest
- Prairie
- Steppe
- Savanna
- Mediterranean
- Dry tropical scrub
- Desert
- Tropical rainforest
- Dry scrub

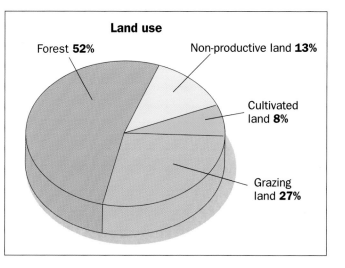

Land use

Forest **52%**
Non-productive land **13%**
Cultivated land **8%**
Grazing land **27%**

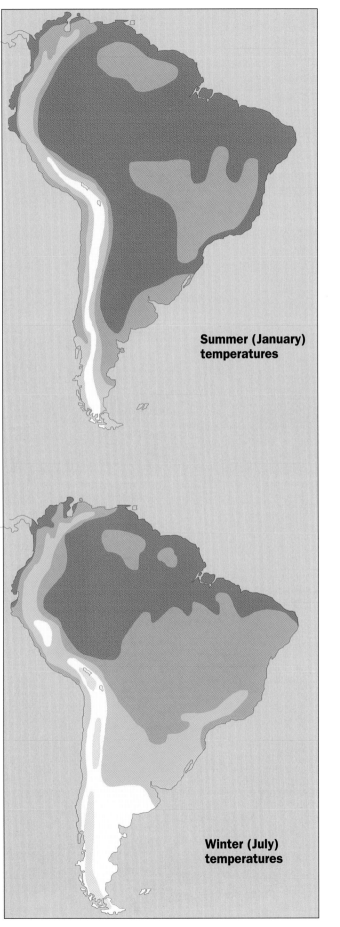

Summer (January) temperatures

Winter (July) temperatures

Temperature
key scale in °C

	−8 to 0
	0 to 8
	8 to 16
	16 to 24
	24 to 32

Range of Climates

Most of South America has a warm climate. This is because much of the land lies in the tropics, with the equator passing through Ecuador, Colombia, and Brazil. High temperatures are accompanied by heavy rainfall, encouraging the growth of the world's largest rainforest, which covers most of equatorial South America.

In the far north, where rain occurs only in one season, the forest merges into the Llanos, a grassy region with scattered trees, like the tropical savanna of Africa.

Southern South America has cooler winters than the tropical lands to the north. The grassy pampas region of northeastern Argentina and Uruguay has a mild, subtropical climate. In winter, cold winds from the Antarctic may bring cold weather and light snow to southern South America.

The pampas region, like the North American prairies, has enough rainfall to support the growth of tall grasses. But to the west, the land becomes drier and the pampas merges into dry steppe. But the driest region is the Atacama Desert, where hundreds of years may pass without any rain. Patagonia, in southern Argentina, is also dry.

Annual rainfall
in mm

	Above 3000
	2000 - 3000
	1000 - 2000
	500 - 1000
	250 - 500
	0 - 250

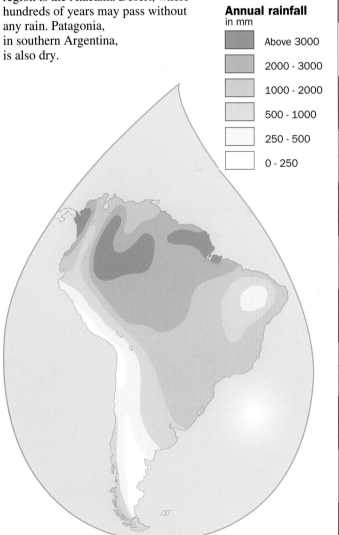

ECOLOGY AND ENVIRONMENT

Western South America, including the high Andes Mountains, is an unstable part of the world, where frequent earthquakes and volcanic eruptions cause great damage. People also cause many problems. The rapid destruction of the Amazon rainforest is a major disaster that may upset the ecology of the whole world. In some dry areas, farmers are clearing the land. Without the protection of plants, the soil is washed away by rain or swept away by winds, leaving bare, infertile ground.

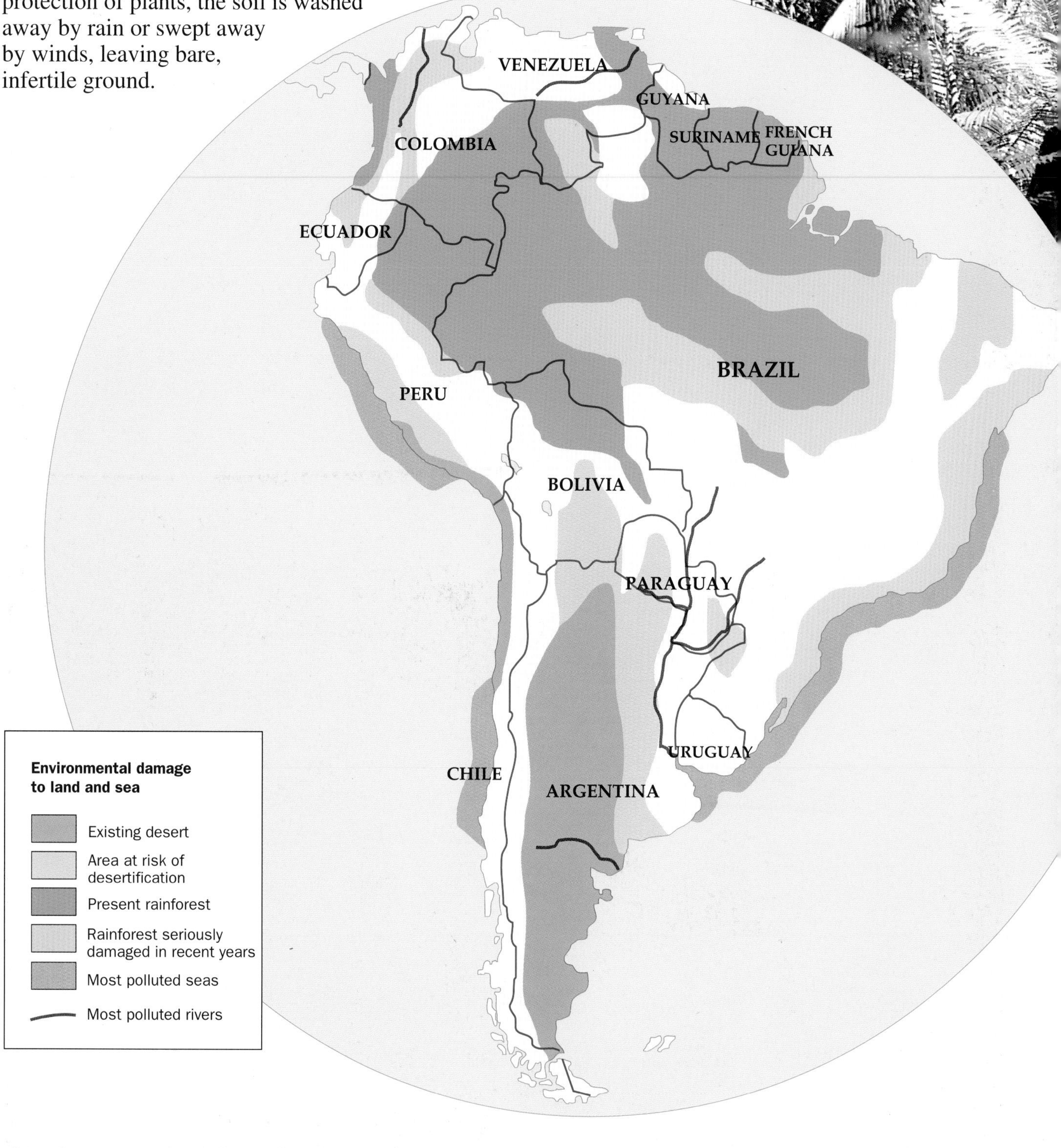

VENEZUELA

GUYANA

COLOMBIA

SURINAME FRENCH GUIANA

ECUADOR

BRAZIL

PERU

BOLIVIA

PARAGUAY

URUGUAY

CHILE

ARGENTINA

Environmental damage to land and sea

Existing desert

Area at risk of desertification

Present rainforest

Rainforest seriously damaged in recent years

Most polluted seas

Most polluted rivers

The destruction of the rainforest is a global problem that requires an international solution.

Damaging the Environment

In 1995, an area of Amazon rainforest the size of Belgium was destroyed by fire. The destruction of rainforest has increased rapidly over the last 30 to 40 years. Some forests are cleared by loggers, who sell the wood they obtain. Other areas are cleared to create new farms and cattle ranches. But the rain soon washes out the minerals from the soil on the cleared land, which often becomes barren and useless. Forest clearance not only causes the extinction of animals and plants, it also threatens the native peoples of the region. Nearly 100 Native American peoples have been wiped out in the last century.

Pollution is caused by factories and cars in the cities, which are growing bigger and bigger as people leave rural areas in the hope of finding jobs. Many remain unemployed and homeless, earning a living in the slums and shanty towns that have grown up around major cities. Lack of food and poor sanitation bring disease and hardship.

Endangered Species

South America's human population is increasing quickly. People need land for homes and for crops, they need wood for building and for fuel, and they need transportation, all of which threaten the plants and animals in large areas that were once unpopulated. The greatest loss of species is occurring in the Amazon Basin, where scientists reckon that many plant and animal species have been destroyed completely, including species that might have proved useful in producing medicines to cure diseases.

Farming in the pampas region of Argentina and Uruguay, as well as sheep farming in Patagonia, has led to a decline in various species, including deer. Rapid population growth in the Andes Mountains and hunting have threatened the spectacled bear and the Andean condor.

Morpho butterfly

Some Endangered Species of South America

Birds
Andean condor
Harpy eagle
Macaws (many species)

Insects
Morpho butterfly

Mammals
Giant otter
Jaguar
Spectacled bear
Uakari
Vicuña

Plants
Alerce cypress
Chilean false larch

Natural Hazards

Massive volcanoes are found throughout the high Andes Mountains. When they erupt, they often cover the land in hot ash. Melted snow mixes with the ash, creating mud flows. Fast-moving rivers of mud surge downwards, submerging villages and towns. Devastating earthquakes are common. They are caused by movements in the huge plates that form Earth's hard outer layers. In South America, the Nazca plate under the southeastern Pacific Ocean is sinking under the South American plate. When it moves, the land shakes. The rocks along the edge of the plate are melted, producing lava.

▲ Active volcanoes

Earthquake zone

Andes

Pacific Ocean

Nazca plate

South American plate

ECONOMY

South America has many natural resources, including minerals, but many of the resources have not been developed. As a result, South America is a poorer continent than North America, Europe, and Australia. The richest countries, which have developed many industries, are Argentina, Brazil, and Chile. Venezuela is also fairly prosperous because of its large oil deposits. The poorest countries are Suriname, Guyana, and Bolivia.

The wealth of South America comes from

- Brazil nuts
- Cocoa
- Coffee
- Cotton
- Fishing
- Forest products
- Fruits
- Gas
- Livestock
- Maize
- Manufacturing
- Mining and minerals
- Oil
- Rubber
- Sheep/wool
- Sugarcane
- Tobacco
- Tourism
- Tropical fruits
- Wheat
- Wines

Only about one-third of the land is cultivated, but farms produce beef, bananas, coffee, sugar, cacao (cocoa), and other products for export. Forest products include timber, Brazil nuts, coconuts, dates, palm oils, and important drugs, such as quinine and curare. Fishing is important, especially along the Pacific coast.

Gross National Product

In order to compare the economies of countries, experts work out the gross national product (GNP) of the countries in US dollars. The GNP is the total value of all the goods and services produced in a country in a year. The pie chart, right, shows that the GNP of Brazil is more than the GNPs of all of the other South American countries combined. However, Brazil's total GNP is only one-tenth of the GNP of the United States. The South American countries with the lowest GNPs are Guyana and Suriname.

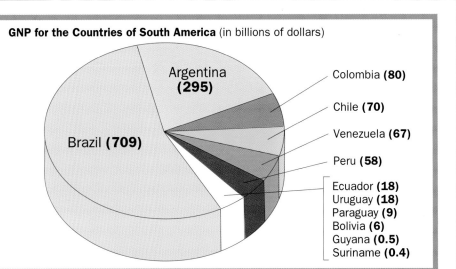

GNP for the Countries of South America (in billions of dollars)

Argentina **(295)**
Brazil **(709)**
Colombia **(80)**
Chile **(70)**
Venezuela **(67)**
Peru **(58)**
Ecuador **(18)**
Uruguay **(18)**
Paraguay **(9)**
Bolivia **(6)**
Guyana **(0.5)**
Suriname **(0.4)**

Per Capita GNPs

Per capita means per head or per person. Per capita GNPs are worked out by dividing the GNP by the population. For example, the per capita GNP of Argentina is US $8,380, which makes it an upper middle-income country. By contrast, Guyana is a low-income economy with a per capita GNP of only $690.

Sources of energy

Venezuela is South America's leading producer of oil, and it ranks among the world's top 10 producers. Argentina and Brazil also produce some oil, but most South American countries have to import oil and other fuels to power their industries.

South America's rivers provide an important source of water power, which is used to produce cheap electricity. For example, most of Brazil's electricity comes from hydroelectric power plants. The Itaipú power plant on the Paraná River on the border of Brazil and Paraguay and the Guri power plant on the Caroni River in Venezuela are among the world's largest.

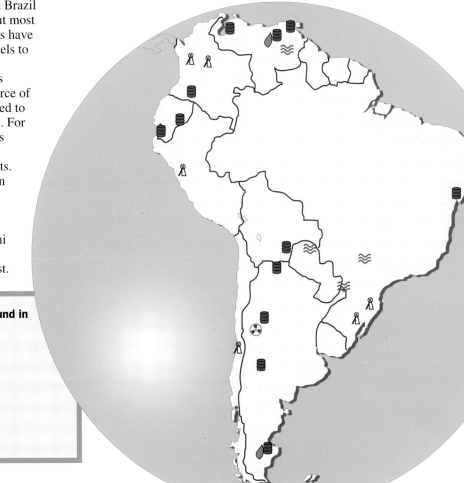

Sources of energy found in South America

- 🛢 Oil
- 💧 Gas
- ≋ Hydroelectricity
- 🅰 Coal
- ☢ Uranium

Politics and History

South America contains 12 independent countries. They are all republics with elected governments and have presidents as their heads of state. The other territories are French Guiana and the British Falkland Islands.

Since most of the countries of South America became independent in the early 19th century, many have suffered from instability. In the 20th century, military leaders have ruled as dictators in several countries.

Francisco Pizarro (1478-1541) led the Spanish force that finally conquered the Incas in 1533.

Great Events

By 6000 B.C. Native Americans had spread throughout South America. They lived as hunter-gatherers, before settling down to farm the land wherever they could. Little is known of the cultures of the ancient forest peoples, but in the Andes the great Inca civilization grew up and left remarkable remains.

Despite their great power, the Incas were defeated in 1532-1533 by a Spanish force. Most of South America was soon occupied by either Spain or Portugal, which took Brazil. The people were forced to adopt the religion and languages of their conquerors. In the early 19th century most countries, inspired by the Venezuelan general Simón Bolívar, and the Argentine general José de San Martin, fought for and achieved freedom from colonial rule.

Wars were frequent, and military groups often overthrew elected governments. Elected leaders, such as Juan Domingo Perón of Argentina, became dictators. The wealthy few held on to their land while millions lived in poverty. Many South American countries are deeply in debt, but political stability is now helping industry to develop and land reforms are reducing poverty.

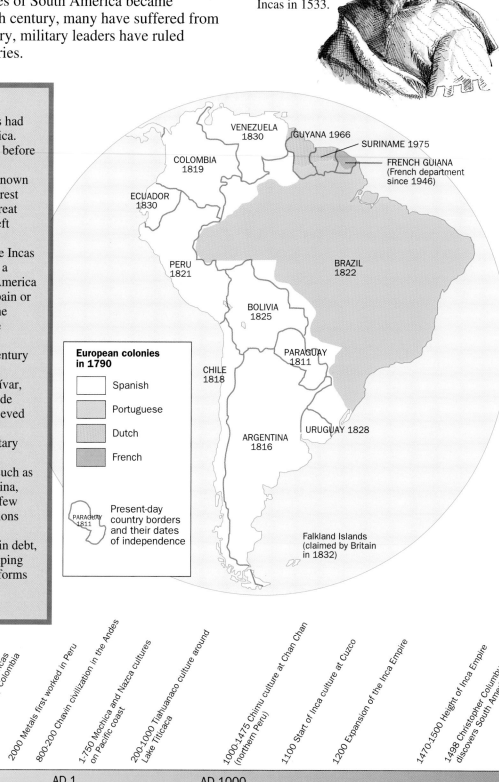

VENEZUELA 1830

GUYANA 1966

SURINAME 1975

FRENCH GUIANA (French department since 1946)

COLOMBIA 1819

ECUADOR 1830

PERU 1821

BRAZIL 1822

BOLIVIA 1825

PARAGUAY 1811

CHILE 1818

ARGENTINA 1816

URUGUAY 1828

Falkland Islands (claimed by Britain in 1832)

European colonies in 1790

☐ Spanish
☐ Portuguese
☐ Dutch
☐ French

PARAGUAY 1811 — Present-day country borders and their dates of independence

Important dates

- 10,000-6000 Hunter-gatherers from the north spread through South America
- 3000 First pottery in Americas made in present-day Colombia and Ecuador
- 2000 Metals first worked in Peru
- 800-200 Chavin civilization in the Andes
- 1-750 Mochica and Nazca cultures on Pacific coast
- 200-1000 Tiahuanaco culture around Lake Titicaca
- 1000-1475 Chimu culture at Chan Chan (northern Peru)
- 1100 Start of Inca culture at Cuzco
- 1200 Expansion of the Inca Empire
- 1470-1500 Height of Inca Empire
- 1498 Christopher Columbus discovers South America

| 10,000 BC | AD 1 | AD 1000 |

Simón Bolívar liberates Colombia, Ecuador, and Venezuela in 1819

Christopher Columbus reaches South America in 1498

Pottery found dating back to 3000 BC

Chibcha culture defeated by Spanish 1525-39

Chan Chan Pre-Inca city of Chimu culture

Machu Picchu great Inca city

Pedro Álvares Cabral claims Brazil for Portugal in 1500

Francisco Pizarro conquers the Inca Empire and begins Spanish rule over the region in 1533. Founds Lima in 1535

Cuzco center of Inca culture

Sucre (Charcas) founded 1538

Inca Empire maximum extent 1470-1500

Potosi main silver-mining center of the Incas discovered by Spanish in 1545

Brasília Founding of new Brazilian capital begins 1956

José de San Martin helps liberate Argentina (1816), Chile (1818) and Peru (1821)

Falkland Islands Argentina invades in 1982 but surrenders after war with UK

Ferdinand Magellan captains the first voyage round the world (1519-21). Magellan Strait named after him

1500 Pedro Álvares Cabral claims Brazil for Portugal

1519-21 Ferdinand Magellan's first circumnavigation of the world. Magellan Strait off southern mainland of South America named after him

1532-3 Francisco Pizarro conquers Peru

1535 Francisco Pizarro founds Lima

1536-8 Spanish defeat Chibcha people of Colombia

1541-2 Francisco de Orellana sails length of Amazon River

1545 Silver mines in Peru discovered by Europeans

1560 Portuguese start sugar cultivation in Brazil

1572 Last Inca leader executed

1693 Gold discovered in Brazil

1808-30 Independence movement in South America creates 10 countries

1864-70 Argentina-Paraguay war

1879 War of the Pacific (Chile, Bolivia, and Peru)

1914 Panama Canal opens; ships no longer have to sail around Cape Horn and South America

1930 Military revolution in Brazil

1932-5 Chaco War between Bolivia and Paraguay

1946 Dictator Juan Domingo Perón comes to power in Argentina

1970-73 Revolution in Chile: Salvador Allende elected president (1970). Overthrown by military dictatorship of Augusto Pinochet (1973)

1974 Eva Perón becomes president of Argentina after the death of her husband

1982 Argentina invades Falkland Islands and surrenders to UK after conflict

1983-9 Democracy restored to Argentina, Brazil, Uruguay, and Chile

1500

AD 2000

37

ANTARCTICA

ANTARCTICA AND ISLANDS

To the east of southern Argentina lie the Falkland Islands, which are geographically part of South America. The southernmost tip of South America is Cape Horn. South of the cape lies a stormy stretch of water called Drake Passage, which is about 640 km (400 miles) wide. This passage separates South America from Antarctica, the fifth-largest continent.

Antarctica is larger than Europe or Australia, but it has no permanent population. This is because it is bitterly cold and mostly covered by a huge ice sheet, up to about 4,800 m (15,700 ft) thick.

ANTARCTICA
Area: about 14,000,000 sq km (about 5,400,000 sq miles)
Highest point: Vinson Massif 5,140 m (16,864 ft)
Population: none permanent

FALKLAND ISLANDS
Area: 12,173 sq km (4,700 sq miles)
Population: 2,600
Capital: Stanley
Government: British overseas territory

Falkland Islands This territory, which consists of two large islands, East and West Falkland, and many small ones, is a British overseas territory, though Argentina claims the islands, which it calls Las Malvinas. In April 1982, Argentine forces invaded the Falkland Islands, but after a brief war Britain regained control.

Scientists visit the South Pole and other parts of Antarctica to carry out research. They drill deep into the ice to collect cores. By counting the layers and identifying chemicals in them, they can see what weather and environmental conditions were like thousands of years ago.

Map labels: SOUTH GEORGIA (UK), FALKLAND ISLANDS (UK), SOUTH ORKNEY ISLANDS (UK), Cape Horn, SOUTH AMERICA, SOUTH SHETLAND ISLANDS (UK), Drake Passage, 90° W, Antarctic Circle, Antarctic Peninsula, Weddell Sea, Ronne Ice Shelf, Vinson Massif 16,864 feet (5,140 m), PACIFIC OCEAN, Amundsen Sea, West Antarctica, South Pole, Ross Ice Shelf, Transantarctic Mts, Ross Sea, Mt Erebus 12,352 feet (3,743 m), 180°

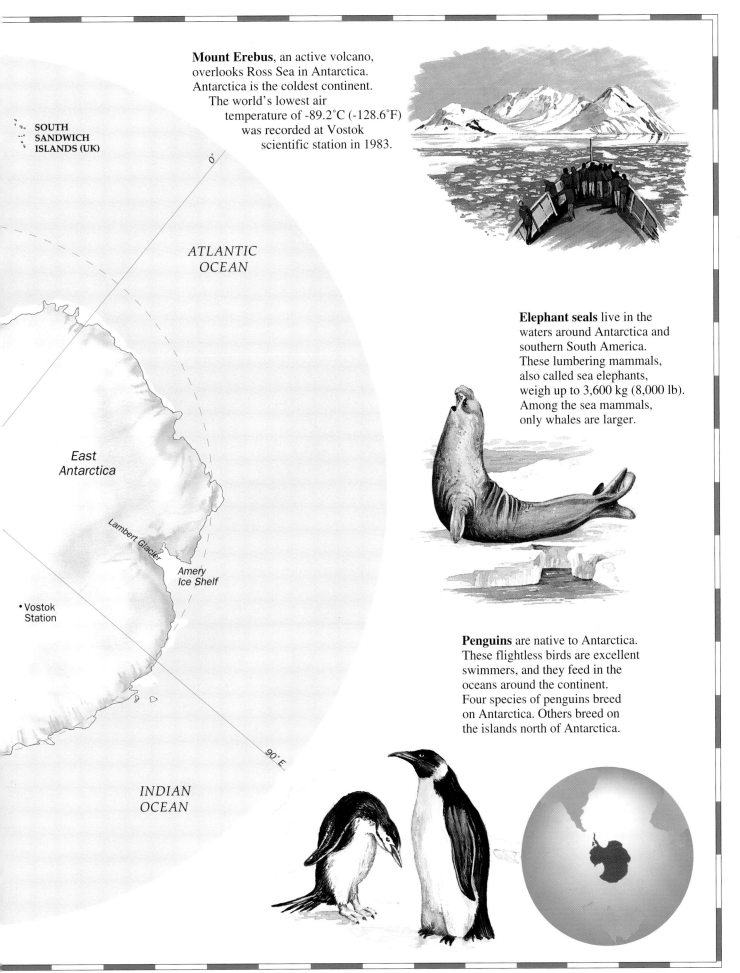

Mount Erebus, an active volcano, overlooks Ross Sea in Antarctica. Antarctica is the coldest continent. The world's lowest air temperature of -89.2°C (-128.6°F) was recorded at Vostok scientific station in 1983.

SOUTH
SANDWICH
ISLANDS (UK)

0°

ATLANTIC
OCEAN

East
Antarctica

Lambert Glacier

Amery
Ice Shelf

• Vostok
Station

90° E

INDIAN
OCEAN

Elephant seals live in the waters around Antarctica and southern South America. These lumbering mammals, also called sea elephants, weigh up to 3,600 kg (8,000 lb). Among the sea mammals, only whales are larger.

Penguins are native to Antarctica. These flightless birds are excellent swimmers, and they feed in the oceans around the continent. Four species of penguins breed on Antarctica. Others breed on the islands north of Antarctica.

THE EXPLORATION OF ANTARCTICA

Antarctica was the last continent to be explored. The British explorer Captain James Cook explored the southern oceans in the 18th century. He crossed the Antarctic Circle but did not sight land. The first men on the continent were probably seal and whale hunters in the early 19th century.

American, French, and British expeditions charted parts of the coast around 1840. One important expedition was led by James Clark Ross. He reached what is now the Ross Sea, where he discovered two volcanoes that he named Erebus and Terror. These were the names of his ships.

The exploration of the interior of Antarctica did not begin until the early 20th century. In 1911, two men set out to reach the South Pole. The Norwegian Roald Amundsen reached the Pole on December 14,1911. He and his companions returned safely. The British explorer Robert Falcon Scott reached the Pole just over a month later, but all the members of his ill-equipped expedition died on the return trip.

Roald Amundsen was the first man to reach the South Pole. The U.S. Amundsen-Scott Station at the Pole is named after him and his British rival, Robert Falcon Scott, who also reached the Pole but died on the way home.

Antarctic explorers
and their expedition dates

Cook 1772-3

d'Urville 1837-40

Wilkes 1838-40

Ross 1839-42

Shackleton 1908

Amundsen 1911-12

Scott 1911-12

Shackleton 1914-6

Fuchs 1957-8

South Georgia

Falkland Islands

SOUTH AMERICA

Weddell Sea

Antarctic Circle

A N T A R C

South Pole

PACIFIC OCEAN

Ross Sea

SOUTHERN OCEAN

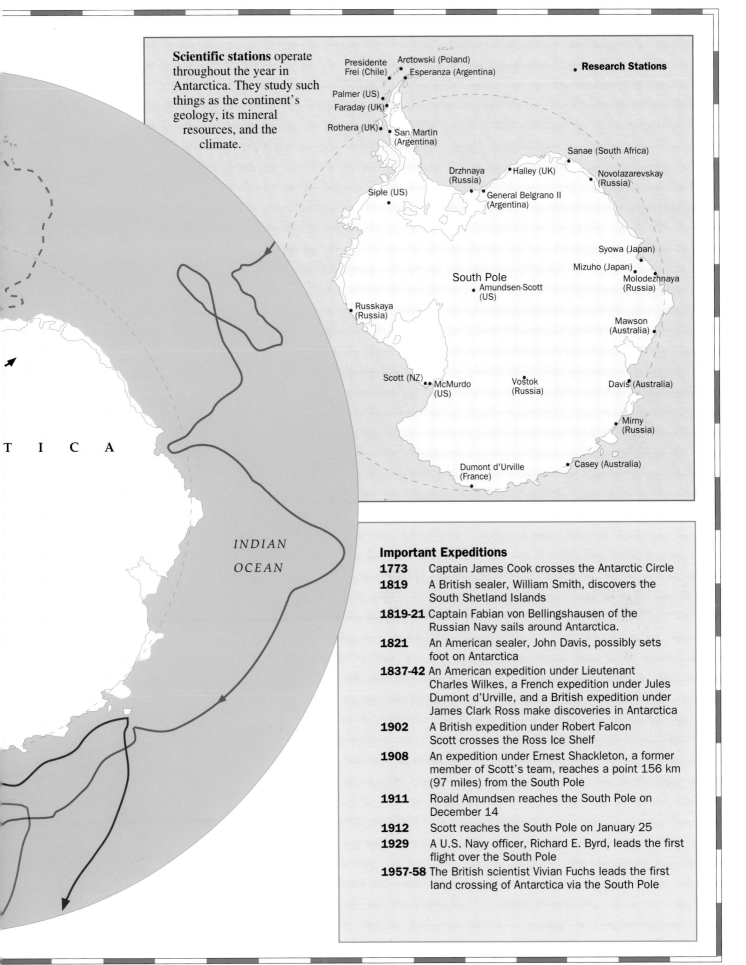

Scientific stations operate throughout the year in Antarctica. They study such things as the continent's geology, its mineral resources, and the climate.

• **Research Stations**

Presidente Frei (Chile)
Arctowski (Poland)
Esperanza (Argentina)
Palmer (US)
Faraday (UK)
Rothera (UK)
San Martin (Argentina)
Drzhnaya (Russia)
Halley (UK)
Sanae (South Africa)
Novolazarevskay (Russia)
Siple (US)
General Belgrano II (Argentina)
Syowa (Japan)
Mizuho (Japan)
Molodezhnaya (Russia)
South Pole
Amundsen-Scott (US)
Russkaya (Russia)
Mawson (Australia)
Scott (NZ)
McMurdo (US)
Vostok (Russia)
Davis (Australia)
Mirny (Russia)
Dumont d'Urville (France)
Casey (Australia)

INDIAN OCEAN

T I C A

Important Expeditions

1773 Captain James Cook crosses the Antarctic Circle

1819 A British sealer, William Smith, discovers the South Shetland Islands

1819-21 Captain Fabian von Bellingshausen of the Russian Navy sails around Antarctica.

1821 An American sealer, John Davis, possibly sets foot on Antarctica

1837-42 An American expedition under Lieutenant Charles Wilkes, a French expedition under Jules Dumont d'Urville, and a British expedition under James Clark Ross make discoveries in Antarctica

1902 A British expedition under Robert Falcon Scott crosses the Ross Ice Shelf

1908 An expedition under Ernest Shackleton, a former member of Scott's team, reaches a point 156 km (97 miles) from the South Pole

1911 Roald Amundsen reaches the South Pole on December 14

1912 Scott reaches the South Pole on January 25

1929 A U.S. Navy officer, Richard E. Byrd, leads the first flight over the South Pole

1957-58 The British scientist Vivian Fuchs leads the first land crossing of Antarctica via the South Pole

ANTARCTICA TODAY

Although Antarctica is a cold and bleak place, it has many resources. For example, coal has been found on the continent. It was formed millions of years ago when Antarctica probably lay close to the equator and had a steamy, hot climate. Since then, Antarctica has slowly moved south to its present position around the South Pole.

Climate and Ice
Temperatures fall dramatically during the Antarctic winter, which lasts from May to August. Icy winds, blowing at high speeds, make it feel even colder. In midsummer in January, temperatures reach 0°C (32°F) on the coast.

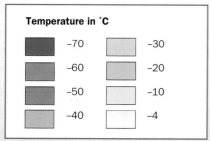

Temperature in °C

–70	–30
–60	–20
–50	–10
–40	–4

In winter the ice shelves extend to form floating pack ice that stretches 1,600 km (1,000 miles) from the coast. In summer the ice breaks up to form flat icebergs, or ice floes. Recently, huge icebergs the size of a small country have broken free. Some scientists think this may be the result of global warming, which may be melting the ice shelves around the continent and causing an increase in snowfall. The partial melting of the Antarctic ice sheet could raise sea levels around the world by between 5 and 20 m (16 to 66 ft), submerging many islands and coastal areas.

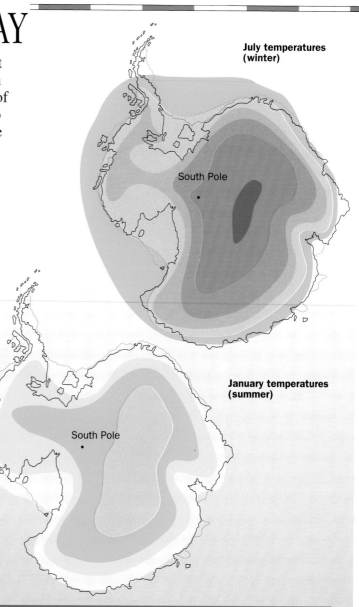

July temperatures (winter)

South Pole

January temperatures (summer)

South Pole

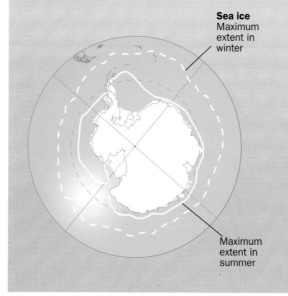

Sea ice
Maximum extent in winter

Maximum extent in summer

The Ozone Hole

In the mid-1980s, scientists in Antarctica discovered that the ozone layer over Antarctica was being thinned by pollution, creating an "ozone hole." By 1998, the "hole" covered an area about three times as large as the United States.

The ozone layer, between 12 and 24 km (7.5 to 15 miles) above the earth, protects the land from the sun's harmful ultraviolet rays, which can cause skin cancer and damage to crops. Many nations now ban the use of the chemicals that are causing the damage.

Exploiting Antarctica

Geologists have discovered deposits of valuable minerals in Antarctica. At present, they are too expensive to mine and ship out from the icy continent. However, when supplies in the rest of the world become scarce, then mining companies might want to exploit them. Many people believe that mining would harm Antarctica so mining there is now banned.

Seven countries have claimed parts of Antarctica in the hope that, one day, they will be able to exploit its resources. However, the claims shown on the map, below, are not recognized in international law. Nations with an interest in Antarctica have signed treaties concerning the continent. For example, the Antarctic Treaty of 1959 states that the continent must be used only for peaceful purposes. It forbids the testing of nuclear weapons and the dumping of nuclear wastes. In 1991, it was also agreed that the exploitation of minerals should be banned for 50 years.

This agreement came into force in 1998.

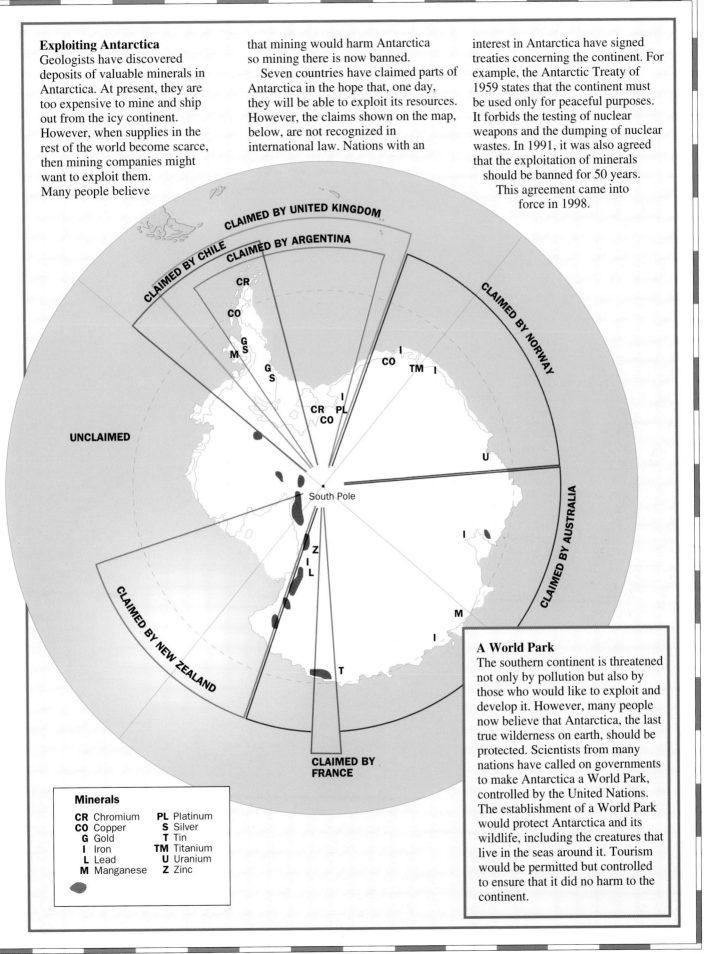

CLAIMED BY UNITED KINGDOM
CLAIMED BY CHILE
CLAIMED BY ARGENTINA
CLAIMED BY NORWAY
CLAIMED BY AUSTRALIA
CLAIMED BY NEW ZEALAND
CLAIMED BY FRANCE
UNCLAIMED

South Pole

Minerals

CR	Chromium	**PL**	Platinum
CO	Copper	**S**	Silver
G	Gold	**T**	Tin
I	Iron	**TM**	Titanium
L	Lead	**U**	Uranium
M	Manganese	**Z**	Zinc

A World Park

The southern continent is threatened not only by pollution but also by those who would like to exploit and develop it. However, many people now believe that Antarctica, the last true wilderness on earth, should be protected. Scientists from many nations have called on governments to make Antarctica a World Park, controlled by the United Nations. The establishment of a World Park would protect Antarctica and its wildlife, including the creatures that live in the seas around it. Tourism would be permitted but controlled to ensure that it did no harm to the continent.

INDEX

Picture credits
Photographs; A S Publishing 8
Bernard Stonehouse 39
The Hutchison Library 5, 6, 7, 9, 13, 15, 17, 23, 26, 32-3
Travel Photo International 19, 21, 25,